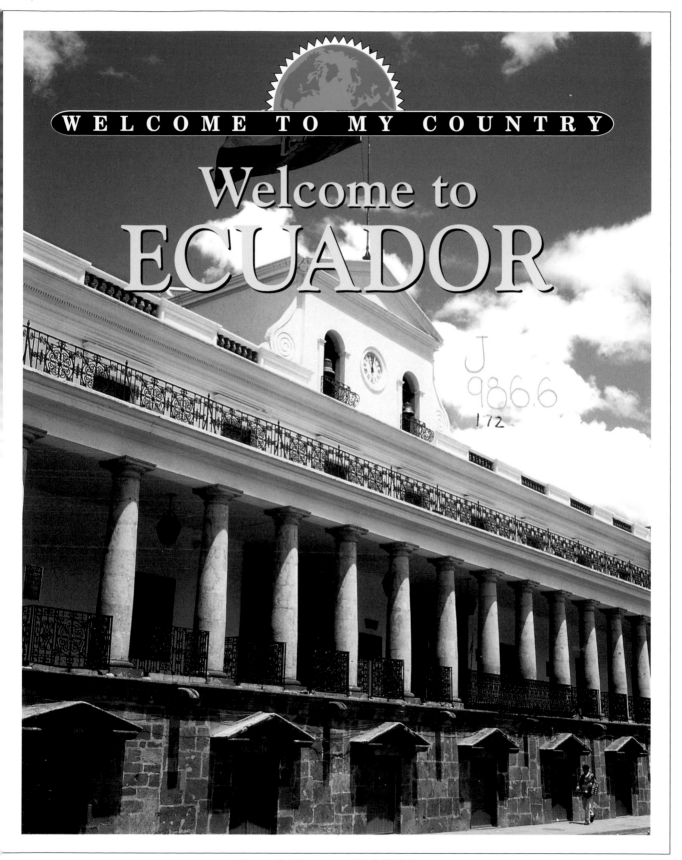

WELCOME TO MY COUNTRY

Welcome to
ECUADOR

Gareth Stevens Publishing
A WORLD ALMANAC EDUCATION GROUP COMPANY

Written by
VIMALA ALEXANDER/AMY S. DANIELS

Edited in USA by
DOROTHY L. GIBBS

Designed by
GEOSLYN LIM

Picture research by
SUSAN JANE MANUEL

First published in North America in 2003 by
Gareth Stevens Publishing
A World Almanac Education Group Company
330 West Olive Street, Suite 100
Milwaukee, Wisconsin 53212 USA

Please visit our web site at:
www.garethstevens.com
For a free color catalog describing
Gareth Stevens' list of high-quality
books and multimedia programs,
call 1-800-542-2595 (USA) or
1-800-387-3178 (CANADA).
Gareth Stevens Publishing's fax: (414) 332-3567.

© **TIMES MEDIA PRIVATE LIMITED 2003**
Originated and designed by
Times Editions
An imprint of Times Media Private Limited
A member of the Times Publishing Group
Times Centre, 1 New Industrial Road
Singapore 536196
http://www.timesone.com.sg/te

Library of Congress Cataloging-in-Publication Data
Alexander, Vimala.
Welcome to Ecuador / Vimala Alexander and Amy S. Daniels.
p. cm. — (Welcome to my country)
Includes bibliographical references and index.
Contents: Welcome to Ecuador! — The land — History —
Government and the economy — People and lifestyle —
Language — Arts — Leisure — Food.
ISBN 0-8368-2543-8 (lib. bdg.)
1. Ecuador—Juvenile literature. [1. Ecuador.]
I. Daniels, Amy S. II. Title. III. Series.
F3708.5.A44   2003
986.6—dc21   2002030676

Printed in Malaysia

1 2 3 4 5 6 7 8 9 07 06 05 04 03

PICTURE CREDITS
Andes Press Agency: 19, 22
Art Directors and Trip Photo Library: 31
Michele Burgess: 3 (bottom), 9, 23, 36
Jan Butchofsky-Houser: cover
Consulate of Ecuador: 15 (top), 15 (center)
Victor Englebert: 3 (center), 6, 25, 29, 35,
    39, 40
Eduardo Gil: 26
Hulton Getty/ Archive Photos:
    15 (bottom), 16
The Hutchison Library: 7, 20, 33
Björn Klingwall: 14
Jason Lauré: 4
North Wind Pictures: 11
Chip and Rosa María Peterson: 5, 12, 17,
    21, 24, 27, 28, 30, 32, 34, 38
Pietro Scozzari: 41
South American Pictures: 1, 3 (top), 8, 13,
    18, 37, 43, 45
Tan Chung Lee: 10
Times Editions: 44 (both)
Topham Picturepoint: 2

Digital Scanning by Superskill Graphics Pte Ltd

Contents

Words that appear in the glossary are printed in **boldface** type the first time they occur in the text.

Welcome to Ecuador!

Although one of South America's smallest countries, Ecuador is a land of great variety. Its name comes from the **equator**, which crosses Ecuador north of its capital city, Quito. The remarkable Galápagos Islands are also part of its geography. Let's learn more about the land and people of Ecuador.

Opposite: These Ecuadorian children are visiting *La Mitad del Mundo* (lah mee-TAHD dehl MOON-doh), or "the middle of the world." This monument marks the position of the equator in Ecuador.

Below: The people of Ecuador are warm and friendly.

The Flag of Ecuador

Ecuador's yellow, blue, and red flag has the nation's **coat of arms** in the center of it. The colors represent abundant crops and fertile land (yellow), the sea and the sky (blue), and the soldiers who fought for independence (red).

The Land

The country of Ecuador, including the Galápagos Islands, has an area of 109,483 square miles (283,560 square kilometers). It borders Colombia to the north and Peru to the east and south. The Pacific Ocean is to the west.

In spite of its small size, Ecuador has four distinct regions. The Coastal Lowland, or *Costa* (KOHS-tah), along the ocean, is an area of flat land about 100 miles (160 kilometers) wide. The

Below: Beautiful Salinas beach, on Ecuador's Pacific shore, is one of the country's many tourist attractions.

Andes Highlands, or *Sierra* (see-EH-rah), is the area surrounding the Andes Mountains. The Andes extend through Ecuador from north to south, dividing the country approximately in half. The Eastern Lowland, or *Oriente* (oh-ree-EHN-teh), is east of the Andes. The largest of Ecuador's regions, this area is mainly a tropical rain forest. The **volcanic** Galápagos Islands, in the Pacific, are Ecuador's fourth region.

Above: Some of the mountains in the Andes range are volcanoes. At 20,561 feet (6,267 meters), the Chimborazo Volcano is the highest peak in Ecuador. The Cotopaxi Volcano, at 19,348 feet (5,897 m), is the world's highest active volcano.

Left: Orchids in many colors and of many varieties grow wild in the rain forest of the Eastern Lowlands.

Climate

Ecuador's climate, although mainly warm and wet, varies at different **altitudes**. Temperatures in the Sierra are normally around 60° Fahrenheit (15° Celsius) all year, but at higher altitudes, that region has mostly ice and snow. The Eastern and Coastal Lowlands are both hot and humid.

Ecuador has two seasons. The rainy season lasts from January into May. The dry season usually begins in June and ends in December.

Plants and Animals

More than eighteen thousand kinds of plants grow in Ecuador. About four thousand kinds grow only in Ecuador, especially on the Galápagos Islands. Many of Ecuador's rain forest plants are used to make medicines.

Included in the country's animal species are every kind of reptile in the world and many kinds of **exotic** fresh-water fish. **Native** Andean condors are one of Ecuador's 1,500 bird species.

Left: Llamas, and similar looking alpacas, are native animals of the Andes Mountains. Ecuadorians value these animals for both their meat and their wool.

History

The first settlers of Ecuador were probably hunters and **gatherers**, but by 3000 B.C., distinct **civilizations** were thriving along the Pacific coast.

In the late 1400s, the Incas of Peru conquered Ecuador's early inhabitants and united them. A **civil war** in 1532, however, weakened the Incan empire, as Princes Huascar and Atahualpa fought for the throne. Atahualpa won.

Below: Located in Cañar Province, the Incan temple of Inga Pirca is the best preserved of all the ruins in Ecuador.

Spanish Rule

Around the time of the Incan civil war, a Spanish army led by Francisco Pizarro came to Peru, searching for gold. Pizarro attacked and defeated the Incas, establishing Spanish rule.

The new government gave pieces of land to Spanish settlers and forced the Indian population to work in the settlers' fields. The Spaniards were expected to defend the land and **convert** the Indians to Christianity.

Above:
In this illustration, Atahualpa and Pizarro are meeting for the first time. After the Spanish conquered the Incas, Pizarro had Atahualpa executed.

Independence

Under the leadership of Napoleon Bonaparte, the French invaded Spain in the early 1800s. When Napoleon's brother Joseph was made the king of Spain, the people of that country and its colonies became very angry.

Spanish settlers in Ecuador rebelled against the French representative. This unrest led South Americans to fight for independence from Spain. Spanish control of Ecuador ended when Simón Bolívar's Venezuelan army won the Battle of Pichincha on May 24, 1822.

Left: A portrait of Simón Bolívar, who led South America's fight for independence, is featured on this mural in Quito.

Left: This picture, from the 1940s, shows a native Ecuadorian Indian in Azuay Province cutting stones for pavement. Even by the mid-1900s, living conditions for Ecuador's Indian population had not improved.

Almost immediately, Ecuador joined Colombia and Venezuela in the confederation of La Gran Colombia. In 1830, when the confederation ended, all three countries became independent.

After independence, the lives of the native Indians, who had become slaves to Ecuador's Spanish settlers, did not change much. From the late 1800s, government leaders such as General José Eloy Alfaro Delgado modernized the country but still neglected the needs of its native peoples.

Modern History

In 1941, a border **dispute** led to a war between Ecuador and Peru. In 1942, the Rio Protocol agreement ended the war, giving the disputed land to Peru, but it did not resolve all of the land issues between the two countries.

President Jamil Mahuad, elected in 1998, finally settled matters with Peru, but he failed to resolve Ecuador's economic problems and, on January 21, 2000, was forced out of office. Vice president Gustavo Noboa replaced him. Noboa's term ends in 2003.

José Eloy Alfaro Delgado (1842–1912)

Serving twice, in 1895 and 1906, as Ecuador's president, Alfaro worked to separate church and state. He also tried to improve conditions for the poor. He was killed by military government supporters in 1912.

José Eloy Alfaro Delgado

Galo Plaza Lasso (1906–1987)

The son of an Ecuadorian president, U.S.-born and educated Galo Plaza Lasso believed in democracy. On becoming president himself, in 1948, he guaranteed the people of Ecuador freedom of speech.

Galo Plaza Lasso

Rosalía Arteaga Serrano (1956–)

As Ecuador's first woman vice president, in 1996, Rosalía Arteaga Serrano, a lawyer, served as the country's president for three days when President Abdalá Bucaram Ortíz was removed from office.

Rosalía Arteaga Serrano

Government and the Economy

Ecuador is a **republic**. Its people elect their government representatives, and the elected president is the head of government. The National Congress, which has 121 elected members, makes the country's laws and appoints judges to its highest court, the Supreme Court. Ecuador's **judicial** system also has a Superior Court and lower courts.

Left: President Gustavo Noboa, with his wife, María Isabel Baquerizo, is waving to people gathered outside the presidential palace in Quito. Noboa became president in 2000. The president of Ecuador serves a four-year term.

Local Government

Ecuador is divided into twenty-two provinces. Except for Galápagos, each province is run by a governor, who is appointed by the president. Galápagos is governed by Ecuador's Ministry of National Defense. Provinces are made up of cities and towns called cantons. Each canton is divided into smaller areas called parishes.

Above: Young Ecuadorians in the city of Esmeraldas are promoting a candidate for a government office. People living in Ecuador's cities and towns can vote directly for some of their local officials.

Economy

Most of the people of Ecuador have jobs in agriculture. Farmers on the Coastal Lowland produce coffee, rice, oranges, bananas, and sugar, mostly for export. Potatoes and corn, for use mainly in Ecuador, are the main crops grown in the Andes Highlands. In recent years, Ecuadorians have been learning modern methods of farming to replace outdated techniques.

Below: Ecuador is one of the world's largest banana producers. Most of the country's bananas are exported to the United States.

Industry and Trade

The discovery of oil in Ecuador, in the 1970s, caused a dramatic increase in manufacturing. Most of the country's manufactured products come from the cities of Quito and Guayaquil.

Although the United States remains Ecuador's main trading partner, recent trade agreements with Venezuela and Colombia have increased the demand for the country's manufactured goods. Italy and Japan also trade with Ecuador.

People and Lifestyle

The people of Ecuador belong to unique groups. **Mestizos** and native Indians are the largest groups. About 10 percent of the population are the descendants of Spanish settlers or other Europeans.

About 9 percent have African ancestors. The lifestyles of these groups are very different from one another. People are either rich or poor. Ecuadorians of European descent are the **elite** group.

Above: Like this family, most of the people who live in the Esmeraldas Province are of African descent.

More than half of the Ecuadorian people are mestizos. About a quarter are native Indians. People in these groups, as well as Afro-Ecuadorians, work very hard to earn a living. Some of the people in these groups even have two or three different jobs.

Many work in farming or construction. Some, however, are professionals in fields such as education and medicine. Government programs are helping to close the gap between rich and poor.

Above: In their spare time, most Ecuadorian men like to get together with friends, sometimes to play cards.

Family Life

Especially in Ecuador's Spanish and
Indian cultures, extended families are
common. Some grandparents, parents,
children, and grandchildren will live
together their whole lives.

In traditional Ecuadorian homes,
men are the main wage earners. In their
free time, however, they do what they
please. Women take care of the home
and the family, but some also have jobs.

Above: The bride
and groom at this
wedding in Otavalo
are dressed in
traditional clothing.

The Roman Catholic tradition of godparenting, known as *compadrazgo* (kohm-pah-DRAHZ-goh), is important in Ecuadorian culture. The parents of a newborn child choose a man and a woman, who are usually close family friends, to be godparents at the child's baptism and to play a role in raising the child. Ecuadorian godparents take this responsibility very seriously.

Below: Ecuador's beautiful city parks are favorite places for families who want to spend a little time outdoors.

Education

All children in Ecuador must attend six years of elementary school and at least three out of six years of secondary, or high, school. Schools are free, but the students must buy books and supplies.

Below: At almost all of the schools in Ecuador, students are required to wear uniforms.

Loyalty to the country is actively encouraged in Ecuadorian schools. Besides patriotic school parades, the Allegiance to the Flag ceremony, or *Jurar la Bandera* (who-RAHR lah bahn-DEH-rah), is held every year.

Ecuador has twelve state-run and five private universities, as well as ten **vocational** schools. These institutions, however, are expensive, so even though students might want higher education, many cannot afford it.

The government offers **literacy programs** for children and adults, especially in **rural** areas. A problem for these programs is that, in poorer rural areas, everyone must work to help support their families.

Above:
Most of the schools in Ecuador are in the cities. Rural schools, like this one in Napo, have fewer students, and their teachers are not well-trained.

Religion

The Roman Catholic Church has played an important role in Ecuador's history. Its involvement in education and social issues has caused many problems between the church and the government. Today, about 95 percent of the population are Roman Catholics, but most of them practice the religion only by observing church holidays.

Below:
Since the 1500s, Catholic priests have lived among Ecuador's native Indians, working to convert them to Christianity.

Some Ecuadorians, especially in the Andes Highlands, have combined native beliefs with Catholic feasts. One of their religious celebrations is the Feast of San Juan, or St. John the Baptist, on June 24. On this day, people dress in beautifully decorated costumes and dance in the streets. This festival, which marks the longest day of the year, dates back to the Incas.

Above: The statue of the Virgin Mary kept at a church in Baños is known to perform miracles. Catholics visit from all over the world to receive the Virgin's blessing.

Language

When the Spanish conquered South America in the 1500s, they taught the people their language. Now, almost all Ecuadorians speak *castellano* (kahs-teh-lee-AH-noh), the **dialect** spoken by the people of Castile, in Spain. Some of the country's native Indians speak Quechua, which was the language of the Incas.

Left:
This sculpture of Juan Montalvo honors him as one of Ecuador's most famous writers. Among his works are *The Seven Treatises* (1882) and *The Chapters That Cervantes Forgot* (1895).

Literature

Juan Montalvo (1832–1889) was one of Ecuador's most important writers. Because of his essays criticizing the politics of Ecuador, Montalvo was forced to leave the country. Other important Ecuadorian writers include Jorge Icaza (1906–1978) and Alicia Yañez Cossio (1929–).

Arts

Spanish settlers constructed awe-inspiring churches and government buildings in the cities of Quito and Cuenca, and artists, such as Miguel de Santiago (c.1630–1706), added **intricate** details. The Guayasamín Museum in Quito exhibits both historical and modern works of art.

Above: Intricate gold artistry adds to the beauty of Sagrario Church in Quito.

Traditional Crafts

Crafts have been part of Ecuadorian life and culture for thousands of years. Archaeologists have found pieces of pottery dating as far back as 3500 B.C. Today, many places in Ecuador have their own traditional crafts. The native people of Otavalo make **tapestries**, sweaters, and other wool products. Ibarra is known for its wood carvings.

Below: Elaborately dressed dolls are popular souvenirs in Otavalo. They are one of many crafts made of wool by the Indians of that region.

Music

Each of Ecuador's cultural groups has its own musical style. The native Indians, in particular, are known for their musical talent. The people of the Andes Highlands play lively folk tunes on instruments such as bamboo flutes, pan pipes, small guitars called *charangos* (chah-RAHN-gohs), and drums. The *cumbia* (KOOM-bee-ah) dance music of Colombia, with its African and Caribbean salsa rhythms, have inspired Ecuador's modern music.

Above: These street musicians are playing Andean tunes on traditional instruments.

The ***marimba*** (mah-REEM-bah) is a traditional instrument of Afro-Ecuadorians in the city of Esmeraldas. It is the main instrument at a dance party called *currulao* (koo-roo-LAH-oh). The people of Ecuador's rain forest play instruments such as turtle shells and bamboo rattles to perform a warrior dance called "Spirit of the Anaconda." This dance tells the story of a large and powerful jungle snake.

Below:
To celebrate the Catholic festival of Corpus Christi, native Indians in Ecuador put on colorful costumes and dance in the streets.

Leisure

Many people in Ecuador spend their leisure time outdoors, in parks or, if they live near the coast, at the beach. Most Ecuadorians also like to watch *telenovelas* (teh-leh-noh-VEH-lahs), which are soap operas about Latin American life. In large cities, wealthy people dine at fine restaurants and watch the latest Hollywood movies.

Left:
Any of Quito's many parks are ideal places for family picnics. The family at this picnic includes a native Indian housekeeper and her children.

Left:
Beauty pageants are as popular in Ecuador as they are in the rest of Latin America. Many of these pageants are part of special holiday celebrations.

Children in Ecuador enjoy outdoor activities such as jump rope, marbles, hopscotch, and other games that do not require much special equipment. They also like to make up games and rhymes. One of these games involves making up new words for popular songs — then singing them!

Sports

Men and boys in Ecuador spend a lot of their leisure time playing soccer, which they call *fútbol* (FOOT-bohl). It is the country's national sport. In 2002, Ecuadorian soccer star Alex

Below:
Ecua-volley (EH-koo-ah-BOH-lay), which is a form of volleyball, is a very popular sport in Ecuador's Andes Highlands.

Aguinaga led the national team to its first World Cup finals at the World Cup championship in Japan and South Korea. Women in Ecuador most often play tennis, basketball, and volleyball. They also enjoy track and field.

Pelota nacional (peh-LOH-tah nah-see-oh-NAHL) is a favorite sport among all Ecuadorians. In this interesting ball game, a team in the middle tries to stop two other teams from hitting the ball back and forth.

Below: These teams are competing on a soccer field that is 10,000 feet (3,048 m) above sea level. Almost every town in Ecuador has a soccer team.

Resorts along Ecuador's Pacific coast offer a variety of water sports, including surfing and scuba diving. Because these sports are expensive, however, only wealthy Ecuadorians and tourists can usually participate.

Festivals

Many of the holidays and festivals in Ecuador are religious celebrations. Some started as Indian traditions. A New Year's Day tradition is burning a **mannequin** at midnight to symbolize the end of the old year and a fresh start in the new year. Celebrations for National Day, on August 10, include parades, food, music, and dancing.

Left: The feast of Corpus Christi, in June, combines elements of both the Catholic faith and Incan harvest festivals. Parades are part of the celebration.

For *Carnaval* (kahr-nah-VAHL), which is usually in February, people dress in colorful costumes to march in parades and attend masked parties. Throwing water balloons at each other is also part of the celebration.

November 2 is *Día de los Muertos* (DEE-ah deh lohs moo-AIR-tohs), or All Soul's Day. On this "day of the dead," Ecuadorians visit the graves of their loved ones.

Above:
To celebrate the Feast of San Juan, the Catholics in Otavalo carry a statue of St. John the Baptist in a procession along city streets.

Food

Fruits, vegetables, and seafood are common foods in Ecuador. Basic foods, some of which are served at almost every meal, include plantains, rice, potatoes, and *yuca* (YOO-kah).

Lunch is the main meal of the day. It usually starts with a bowl of soup and includes a salad, a main dish of meat with rice or potatoes, and

Below: Seafood dishes, such as *ceviche* (seh-VEE-cheh), are popular in Ecuador's coastal region. Ceviche is raw fish and onions soaked in lemon sauce.

a dessert. Breakfast and dinner are smaller, lighter meals. For snacks, Ecuadorians like to eat *empanadas* (ehm-pah-NAH-dahs), which are hot pastries filled with meat or cheese.

Many kinds of *ají* (ah-HEE), or chili peppers, grow in Ecuador. Ají is used to spice up almost every meal. People make ají sauces by pounding chilis and mixing them with water and other seasonings.

Above: Healthy and inexpensive plantains can be fried, boiled, or baked and are made into everything from chips to desserts.

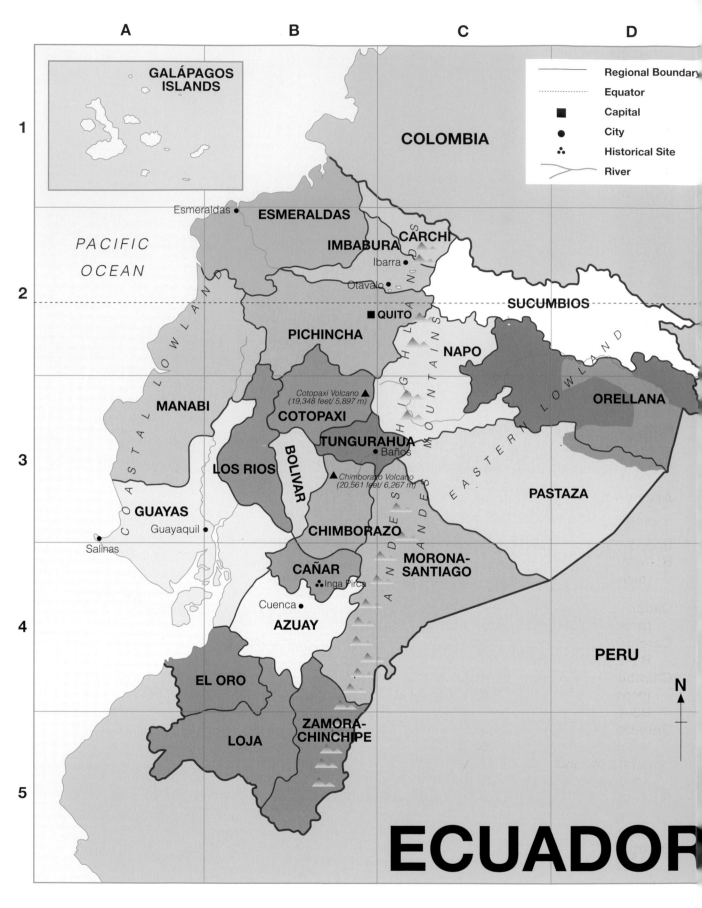

GALÁPAGOS
ISLANDS

Regional Boundary
Equator
■ Capital
● City
⁝ Historical Site
River

COLOMBIA

Esmeraldas ● **ESMERALDAS**

CARCHI

PACIFIC
OCEAN

IMBABURA

Ibarra ●

Otavalo ●

SUCUMBIOS

■ QUITO

PICHINCHA

NAPO

MANABI

Cotopaxi Volcano ▲
(19,348 feet/ 5,897 m)

COTOPAXI

ORELLANA

TUNGURAHUA

Baños ●

LOS RIOS

BOLIVAR

▲ Chimborazo Volcano
(20,561 feet/ 6,267 m)

PASTAZA

GUAYAS

Guayaquil ●

CHIMBORAZO

Salinas ●

CAÑAR

⁝ Inga Pirca

**MORONA-
SANTIAGO**

Cuenca ●

AZUAY

PERU

EL ORO

N

**ZAMORA-
CHINCHIPE**

LOJA

ECUADOR

COASTAL LOWLAND

HIGHLAND

ANDES MOUNTAINS

EASTERN LOWLAND

Above: Restaurants and shops line a busy street in Guayaquil, Ecuador's largest city.

Andes Highlands
C2–C4
Andes Mountains
C2–B5
Azuay
(province) B4

Baños B3
Bolivar
(province) B3

Cañar
(province) B4
Carchi (province)
B1–C2
Chimborazo
(province)
B3–B4
Chimborazo
Volcano B3
Coastal Lowland
A4–B2
Colombia B1–D2
Cotopaxi (province)
B2–B3
Cotopaxi
Volcano B3
Cuenca B4

Eastern Lowland
C3–D2
El Oro (province)
A4–B4
Esmeraldas (city) B2
Esmeraldas
(province) B1–B2

Galápagos Islands
A1
Guayaquil B3
Guayas (province)
A3–B4

Ibarra C2
Imbabura (province)
B2–C2
Inga Pirca (ruins)
B4

Loja (province)
A5–B4
Los Rios
(province) B3

Manabi (province)
A3–B2

Morona-Santiago
(province)
B4–C3

Napo (province)
C2–C3

Orellana (province)
C2–D3
Otavalo C2

Pacific Ocean
A5–B1
Pastaza (province)
C3–D3
Peru A4–D2

Pichincha (province)
B2–C2

Quito B2

Salinas A3
Sucumbios
(province)
C2–D2

Tungurahua
(province)
B3–C3

Zamora-Chinchipe
(province)
B4–B5

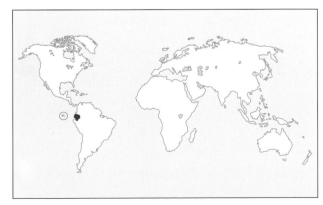

Quick Facts

Official Name Republic of Ecuador

Capital Quito

Official Language Spanish

Population 13,447,494 (2002 estimate)

Land Area 109,483 square miles (283,560 square km)

Provinces Azuay, Bolivar, Cañar, Carchi, Chimborazo, Cotopaxi, El Oro, Esmeraldas, Galápagos, Guayas, Imbabura, Loja, Los Rios, Manabi, Morona-Santiago, Napo, Orellana, Pastaza, Pichincha, Sucumbios, Tungurahua, Zamora-Chinchipe

Major Cities Quito, Guayaquil

Highest Point Chimborazo Volcano 20,561 feet (6,267 m)

Main Religion Roman Catholicism

Important Holidays New Year's Day (January 1)
Carnaval (February)
Battle of Pichincha (May 24)
Corpus Christi (June)
National Day (August 10)
All Soul's Day (November 2)
Christmas Day (December 25)

Currency U.S. dollar

Opposite: This monument in Guayaquil honors Simón Bolívar and José de San Martín.

Glossary

altitudes: heights above sea level.

civil war: a war between sections of the same country or different groups of citizens within that country.

civilizations: societies that have highly developed cultures and governments and established, written records of their histories.

coat of arms: a specially designed symbol, usually in the form of a crest or a shield, that represents and identifies a specific family, group, institution, or geographic region.

convert (v): to change from one faith or religious belief to another.

dialect: the form of a language used in a particular region or area of a country.

dispute: an argument, quarrel, or struggle based on a disagreement.

elite: the richest, best educated, or most powerful people in a society.

equator: an imaginary line around the middle of Earth at an equal distance from both the North and South Poles.

exotic: unusual or very different from most of the same kind.

gatherers: people who harvest, or gather, what nature provides in order to survive.

intricate: detailed or complex.

judicial: related to the enforcement of justice by courts of law.

literacy programs: planned activities that teach reading and writing.

mannequin: a life-size model of a human figure.

marimba **(mah-REEM-bah):** an African or Central American type of xylophone.

mestizos: people who have a mixed Spanish or European and native American Indian ancestry.

native: belonging to a certain place by being born there.

republic: a nation in which the citizens elect their own lawmakers.

rural: related to the countryside.

tapestries: pieces of cloth that have a pattern or a picture woven into them.

vocational: related to an occupation, profession, or skilled trade.

volcanic: produced by or coming from a volcano.

yuca **(YOO-kah):** a potatolike tropical plant that has a starchy root and can be eaten.

More Books to Read

Children of Ecuador. Through the Eyes of Children series. Connie Bickman (Abdo & Daughters)

The Children of the Ecuadorean Highlands. World's Children series. Barbara Beirne (Carolrhoda Books)

Francisco Pizarro. Groundbreakers series. Ruth Manning (Heinemann Library)

"Galapagos" Means "Tortoises." Ruth Heller (Sierra Club Juveniles)

The Incas. See Through History series. Tim Wood (Viking Children's Books)

Llamas. Early Bird Nature Books series. Dorothy Hinshaw Patent (Lerner)

Lost Treasure of the Inca. Peter Lourie (Boyds Mills Press)

Nilo and the Tortoise. Ted Lewin (Scholastic)

Up a Rainforest Tree. Amazing Journeys series. Carole Telford and Rod Theodorou (Heinemann Library)

Videos

Ecuador. Hello! From Around the World series. (Library Video)

Experience Ecuador & the Galapagos Islands. (Questar)

Treasure of the Andes. (Educational Broadcasting Corporation)

Volcanoes & Rainforests. Going Places series. (MPI Home Video)

Web Sites

www.clemetzoo.com/rttw/condor/allabt.htm

www.ips.uiuc.edu/sao/photopages/ecuadorphoto.html

www.kent.wednet.edu/KSD/SB/Ancient/Inca.html

www.peacecorps.gov/kids/world/iac/ecuador.html

Due to the dynamic nature of the Internet, some web sites stay current longer than others. To find additional web sites, use a reliable search engine with one or more of the following keywords to help you locate information on Ecuador. Keywords: *Andes, Galápagos, Incas, llama, marimba, Juan Montalvo, Otavalo, Quechua, Quito.*

Index